AIVAN LEEDS

SLOW JOGGING

The Ultimate Jogging Guide For Beginners, Learn Useful Tips on How to Jog the Right Way to Effectively Lose Weight

Descrierea CIP a Bibliotecii Naţionale a României
AIVAN LEEDS
SLOW JOGGING. The Ultimate Jogging Guide For Beginners, Learn Useful Tips on How to Jog the Right Way to Effectively Lose Weight / Aivan Leeds – Bucharest: Editura My Ebook, 2021
ISBN

AIVAN LEEDS

SLOW JOGGING

The Ultimate Jogging Guide For Beginners, Learn Useful Tips on How to Jog the Right Way to Effectively Lose Weight

My Ebook Publishing House
Bucharest, 2021

CONTENTS

Jogging to Lose Weight

Anyone who is trying to lose weight needs to engage in some kind of aerobic exercise in order to boost the metabolism to burn calories faster. Although a brisk walk will suffice, many people are more comfortable with jogging and feel it works better for them. Making the choice to jog during weight loss will not only help you lose weight but will also help you get into the routine of exercising, a move that will help you keep the weight off when you have reached your goal weight. The ideal exercise for weight loss is a combination of aerobic and resistance exercise - jogging combined with some weight lifting routines.

Getting into the habit of jogging is not a difficult one for most people, but if you have never been one to exercise, it may come as a shock at first. You do not want to try to jump right into a long jogging workout but rather begin slowly and work your way up to where you want to be. Do not rush to reach the amount of time you wish to spend jogging but let your body guide you and let you know when you are ready. If you allow your body to be your guide, it will be much easier to work into a jogging routine without all of the discomfort.

In order to achieve the ultimate weight loss, you want to make jogging part of your routine but not the only exercise you perform. Although aerobic exercise is what helps you burn calories, resistance exercise helps you build lean muscle mass which burns fan faster. Therefore the perfect routine is a combination of aerobic and resistance exercise. Of course, if you can't do the resistance routines for health reasons, then certainly you can obtain the benefits from jogging but you may find it takes longer to accomplish. However, any kind of exercise you can perform will certainly help you lose weight and keep it off after you have reached your goal weight. You have to remember you will need to keep it up in order to maintain your weight loss. You cannot stop once you have reached your goal weight and expect to maintain the results.

Do not overdo your jogging in an attempt to lose weight faster. Though you may accomplish that goal, it will be at the cost of your health. Working your muscles too hard even in jogging can cause your muscles and cartilage to become damaged thus preventing you from doing many activities including jogging.

Choose a Jogging Trail that is Away from Traffic

Although you want to job in places that are well populated you also want to stay away from traffic. Do not choose high traffic roads to jog even if you are on the side of the road facing traffic. There is always the possible that a car or truck will veer off the road and hit you or maybe just pull off the road with mechanical problems and fail to see you. If you choose roads that have a high traffic volume, choose one that has a sidewalk or a shoulder that is far enough off the main road for you to be safe.

In addition to the potential for being hit jogging in a high traffic area, is the possibility of being mugged or even kidnapped as you jog alongside the road. You can avoid those possibilities by making sure you are on the sidewalk or far enough away from the highway that someone would have to stop the car and get out in order to pull you into the car. Safety is a very important issue for joggers and one that you should not take lightly. Jogging is a healthy activity for the body but you also have to make sure you perform it with your personal safety in mind.

One of the best ways to make certain you are in a well-lit area that is well populated is in a business area. Keep in mind that not all business sections will follow this pattern, so you still have to be careful where you go. For example, factories and warehouses are not the safest places to be because even though people may be working, they are usually secluded and unable to see what is going on outside. The best places are round stores where customers come and go at all times rather than restaurants or movie theaters where customers are frequently inside rather than outside.

The key to making jogging a healthy activity is to make certain you are aware of the surroundings where you jog and to be attentive to your surroundings. Do not make yourself a target by being preoccupied with your own thoughts or with a music player. Although it may help pass the time while you are jogging it also puts your safety in danger and makes you vulnerable to a surprise attack by someone you neither saw nor heard.

Choosing Proper Clothing for Jogging

One of the most important things to consider when jogging is your clothing, especially the type of shoes you wear. You want something that is comfortable and that is specifically for running or jogging. You can also choose cross trainers if you desire, but it is better to have something with cushioning such as the Nike Air and similar shoes. The cushioning in the shoes will help prevent any hard landing on your feet as well as allowing airflow through your feet to prevent damage to the feet, knees and legs. If you have to make sacrifices due to budgetary concerns do not do it with your shoes. The shoes are the most important part of your jogging clothing when it comes to preventing injury.

Your outer clothing is also important because you do not want to be too cold or too warm. In the warmer months, you can certainly choose shorts and a short sleeve or sleeveless top or shirt, but you also want to make sure, if you are jogging during the daylight hours to protect your skin from the sun with sun block that has an SPF of at least 15. You also want to wear a sun hat or cap that protects your head and prevents heat stroke or heat exhaustion. During colder months, you will want to choose, either sweat pants or track pants. Never go out jogging wearing short sleeves when it is cold outside. You may feel you will stay warm because of your exercise but the reality is that the sweat from your body mingling with the cold air makes a perfect environment for illness.

If you are going jogging during a time when there is likely to be a severe change in temperature you may want to take along a light jacket and tie it around your waist while you are jogging. In the event the temperature drops substantially you will be able to put your jacket on and shield yourself from the cold. Use a waist pack to carry any money or keys you need rather than attempting to carry even a small purse that a mugger can easily take. Better yet, put your money and keys in your pocket where they are out of view from people. The less opportunity you provide for criminal acts the least likely you are to become a victim.

Choosing Well Lit Places to Jog

Jogging may be your exercise of choice but you also want to make sure you exercise precautions when you job. This is especially important for women although men are certainly not immune to acts of violence. One of the most important things to remember is to always job in well-lit areas. If you go to a park, stay away from any areas that are secluded such as bushes and trees. You want to choose well-lit areas so you can see what is going on and are on the lookout for any strangers and anyone who looks suspicious.

If the area where you customarily jog does not have, lights avoid that area or take your own. You never want to take the chance of someone jumping at you suddenly and you are not able to see the person. No matter where you live you do not want to take a chance - even, high-class neighborhoods have criminals or criminals come in from other areas. You do not want to take a chance of being another statistic because you failed to exercise reasonable precautions by making sure to job in a well-lit area.

Besides avoiding criminal activity, it is also a good idea to jog in a well-lit area so that you are able to follow the trail you have set for yourself. If you are jogging after dark, it is very easy to lose track of where you are going, especially if you are concentrating more on your jog than on where you are going. Certainly, it is preferable to job while it is still light, but if that is not possible because of work commitments or other valid reason, make sure you can see where you are going and who might be hiding in the shadows.

The best rule to follow when jogging is to exercise caution and know where you are going. Never choose areas you do not know even if they are well lit and appear to be populated. Nighttime is not the time to learn new places to go or attempt to decide if an area is bright enough for you to see anyone who may come out from the shadows. There are many would-be attackers that are looking for those who have failed to exercise precautions and are therefore very vulnerable and an easy prey. Do not be one of the unlucky ones.

Creating Your Own Jogging Trail

For those who live in rural areas or even suburban areas with a good deal of land, you might want to consider creating your own jogging trail. It does not have to be anything fancy, and you can choose to use grass or dirt at your preference. Some people may even find it helpful to use AstroTurf or a similar product - "fake grass" instead of the real thing. The choice you make is yours but you want to make sure the design and space meets your needs. Check it before you begin so that you make sure you allow enough space because once you finish there is no going back without redoing the entire jogging trail.

Another possibility for those who live in a neighborhood with a lot of open land is to obtain permission to create a jogging trail on a piece of that open land. In many cases, the open land belongs to the state or the county, and for a good cause, they may even do the construction and foot the cost for you if enough people are interested. Even if they will not finance the project, all you need is permission to use the land for the jogging trail. It is something that would be a benefit to the community as a whole much as a park is beneficial to the children of a community.

Sometimes it is not necessary to obtain permission to create a jogging trail; it depends where you want to place it. Certainly if it is part of your property, you will not need permission as long as you stay within the bounds of your own property and do not create any obstructions that would prevent public access to water or sewer lines. A project would not only be beneficial but inexpensive. Having your own jogging trail would also mean you do not have to worry about your safety in a remote area and would make the activity more enjoyable for you. In addition, you would never have to worry about going out in the weather or wondering where you could go to jog.

If you are considering creating your own jogging trail, you might want to get together with a neighbor and perhaps build one the two of you can share. This project can be a benefit to more than one person and would help both families become healthier by engaging in a mutual exercise.

Developing a Jogging Routine

Before you begin jogging, you want to develop a routine that combines jogging with walking or running. Although jogging is fine in itself, a combination of other aerobic exercise is much better on the body.

Jogging is a good way to develop a slow and rhythmic pace but it can also be bad on the calves and knees if you are not careful. That is one reason it's better to try to combine jogging with running or walking. If possible, try to do your jogging on a soft - or at least smooth - surface. The softer the surface on which you jog the easier it will be on your legs. Of course, it can be difficult to jog on grass unless it is solid, so the time of year you are attempting to jog will have a huge impact on where you can jog.

You want to develop a routine that does not cause you to run the risk of injury. That means stopping when your body has told you that you have had enough. Even if you develop a routine that calls for one hour per day, let your knees and legs be the guide. If they are beginning to hurt, do not continue insisting you are going to meet your goals. Continuing when you are experiencing pain can be detrimental to your health. The idea of jogging is to develop and participate in a healthy activity that allows you to burn calories and increase your heart rate. That does not mean you have to cause health problems for yourself in the meantime by any means. You can gradually build to a pace your body can tolerate - there is no need to do it all in one day or even a week. While some people may be able to develop a good routine in a week, it may take others a couple of weeks or even a month.

The level of tolerance for each person will be different which is why you cannot develop your routine based upon any general set of rules. You also cannot follow someone else's guidelines about how long you should jog or how long it should take you to be able to reach your ultimate goal. No two people are alike and you have to follow your own body and tolerances. If you attempt to push yourself beyond your body's tolerances, you will defeat the purpose of your jogging routine.

Don’t Overdo it

Sometimes we are tempted to overdo things in the exercise department. With resistance exercises the worse you’re going to do is have some sore muscles for a few days - in most cases anyway - but if you overdo it when you’re jogging you run the risk of damaging your knees or calves. The consistent pressure on the balls of the feet and the knees will eventually take a toll on those parts of your body if you are not careful. That means not to attempt to jog for hours at a time even if you may split it up throughout the day. You want to set aside perhaps an hour a day for jogging and only if you are able to do so.

When you first start jogging you want to begin slowly and gradually increase the amount of time you spend jogging. If you find your legs or knees are hurting stop jogging. Do not attempt to rest and go back later but stop for the day. When your body becomes used to the new routine you will then be able to spend more time jogging during the day - perhaps even stop when you begin to hurt and return later.

However, you do not want to attempt to do this until your body including your legs, knees and feet become used to jogging.

If you want to continue with your exercise routine when you knees and legs are beginning to hurt or tire, you might be able to resort to brisk walking rather than jogging. Walking will put less stress on your legs and knees and will be safer when you are no longer able to jog. Even walking at a leisurely pace is acceptable at this stage in order to prevent injury. The idea is to learn how to exercise on a regular basis, not wear out your body parts so that you are no longer able to do the things you are used to doing.

Jogging can be a fun and healthy activity if you make sure you let your body tell you when it has had enough. There is nothing any worse than continuing to exercise long after your body has told you it has had enough. Although you may set a period for your exercise, you want your body to be the final judgeof when you have had enough for the day.

Dress for the Weather When Jogging

Although you want to dress so that you do not become overheated, you also want to dress for the weather. Even if you feel you will become sufficiently warm, do not go outside in cold weather wearing shorts and a tee shirt. The combination of the cold outside and your sweat from jogging will cause you to become chilled and creates the potential for illness. Instead, you want to wear a sweat suit or tracksuit during cold weather. You may feel you will be overly war but in reality, you will not become warm enough to justify wearing shorts in the middle of the winter.

Although you may be one of the people who is tempted to jog no matter what kind of weather you might encounter keep in mind that your purpose is to perform healthy exercise, and you cannot do that if you insist on jogging when there is snow, ice, sleet or freezing rain. That may sound like common sense, but if you look outside you will find at least one or two people jogging during extreme weather. Even in the summer months, it can be detrimental to your health to job in the rain because the combination of sweat and rain can still give you a chill and cause a summer cold.

The worst times to jog in terms of clothing are likely to be spring and fall because of the potential for a severe change in temperatures as the sun goes down. You need to be ready for these changes and not assume you can wear the same jogging outfit at any time of the day or evening. Always be aware of weather changes throughout the day and adjust your clothing accordingly. The inclination to wear shorts when you jog no matter what they weather may be is one that causes many people to become ill.

Use common sense and proceed with caution. Dress for the weather and do not go jogging if you arealready sick. Although it may be a healthy activity, it can cause those with a low immune system to become very ill if they are not careful. Remember, it does not take much to break down your immune system - one of the easiest ways to do that is lack of sleep or general fatigue. In addition, activities suchas smoking also wear on the immune system and make a person more susceptible to colds and other illnesses.

Is Jogging Healthy for Everyone?

Although jogging is a healthy form of exercise, it is definitely not for everyone. Some people have health conditions that prevent them from jogging such as knee problems or even heart problems. There are also those who have respiratory problems that may not want to participate in jogging, at least not during the summer when they are most likely to be overheated and possibly have an attack. Although most people are physically able to jog, you should always check with your doctor if you have any physical condition that might make it unsafe. You want to make the right choice or jogging will not improve your health. In fact, if you undertake jogging when you have poor health it will defeat the purpose.

Anyone who is not able to do any kind of running or at least brisk walking should probably not participate in jogging. That also includes anyone who has back, knee or leg problems because the additional stress can possibly create more problems. That does not mean those people should not participate in any kind of exercise but they should choose something their doctor recommends and that will consider their condition. You do not want to create more health problems for yourself by participating in an activity that your body cannot handle. The choice you make will allow you to continue living an active lifestyle but if you make the wrong choice, you are liable to find you are unable to do thesame things you used to be able to do. It is important to know your limitations and accept them for what they are rather than trying to overcome them.

When we were young, we never let things get us down and made it a point to overcome any limitations that may have presented themselves. As we get older, we have to work around those limitations. That means you do not try to do things that you know are impossible or will cause injury to any body parts. That includes jogging and any other activities that you may no longer be able to perform. It is easy enough to find something else - brisk walking or leisurely walking for instance. There is no need to be stress on your body because you thought you could still jog about you had knee surgery. Be reasonable - there are enough activities for everyone who is interested in improving their health with aerobicexercise.

Is Jogging Safe for Heart Patients?

Although heart patients are encouraged to walk, is it safe for them to jog? After all, there is only minimal difference between brisk walking and jogging. The thing to remember is that different patients have different degrees of heart problems. It is important to remember that the cardiologist is the one who knows fully how serious a patient's condition is. While one patient may be perfect fine with jogging, another one may only allow brisk or even leisurely walking. The final answer falls under knowing how much stress an individual patient's heart can take based on the health of that patient only.

Regardless of how well you may feel, never undertake jogging without the permission of your doctor. There may be any number of reasons your doctor does not want you to jog, especially if you have undergone heart surgery. It takes time to heal, and only your doctor can determine at one point you are healed enough to participate in jogging. It is by far more strenuous than just walking, so you do not want to jog until and unless your doctor approves. An exercise that is as healthy as jogging is not necessarily healthy for everyone and thus may cause health problems rather than create a healthier body.

What if your doctor does not tell you whether you can jog or not after a heart attack or heart surgery, like any diet or exercise routine, do you participate unless you consult your doctor first. You need to speak to your doctor and let him know the exercise routine you wish to perform, and he will let you know if you can do it. If he tells you no, you are free to question his reasons but under no circumstances should you make your own decision about it. Remember, the doctor has all of your health records including EKGs, so you need to trust his best judgment. Even if he tells you that you are limited to walk leisurely for the rest of your life, you must accept that he is doing what is best for you.

Even if you have not had a heart attack but have a heart condition that may have an effect by jogging, always ask your doctor before you participate. Only your doctor knows the factors that may affect your heart condition and/or make it worse. Do not be fooled into thinking jogging is healthy for everyone because there are conditions under which hat may not be the case.

Is There a Right or Wrong Way to Jog?

Good solid question, right, how do you jog? Is there a right or wrong way to jog? Although some might say it makes no difference, others may disagree with that. Everyone has his or her own personal preference about different things, and when those preferences are different from what others may do, it means the other person is “wrong.” Is that actually true? No, it is not necessarily true, but in the eyes of the person doing things differently, it is indeed the wrong way of doing whatever activity it was.

Whether it is jogging, running, or even vacuuming the floor, some people believe there is a right and wrong way to do it.

In retrospect, jogging involves the slow, rhythmic movement of a run, more like a trot or gallop of a horse than an actual run. Because of its slower pace, people who cannot run can usually jog. That is not always the case; there are exceptions such as heart patients and others who may not have the ability to perform any activity beyond that of a brisk or leisurely walk. For those who have the pleasure of being able to jog, they will develop their own way of doing it, and there is actually no right or wrong way to do it. The key issue is being up to keep up a slow steady pace but there is no right or wrong way except in the minds of some perfectionists.

No matter what you teach people about jogging, they are still going to find their own methodology, something that works for them. The choice is personal and as long as the result is the same there is little relevance to the reasoning or methodology that separates one person's style from another. There will always be different ways to jog based on a person's personal preference and even of their weight and body build. Some people just find one way of jogging easier than another with some even choosing to alternate between jogging and brisk walking and even running. It is not your style of jogging that will make a difference in your health but rather your perseverance in doing it. Choosing to remain healthy by participating in jogging as your exercise of choice will provide you with more years of good health than those who choose to lead a sedentary lifestyle.

Jogging and Walking: the Perfect Combination

If you enjoy both jogging and walking or maybe find you cannot jog for very long at a time, you might want to consider a combination of both. You can start out jogging and as you begin to tire or feel pain inyour knees or legs, switch to brisk walking. Many health professionals will even tell you that brisk walking is better for you than running, so substituting walking during your daily jog is not going to minimize the health benefits of jogging. In fact, you will find that you can increase the length of time you can participate when you combine the two activities instead of trying to jog o walk during the entire time.

One reason it is much more beneficial to combine jogging with walking is that each activity has certain limitations in terms of health benefits. For example, jogging too much can cause problems with your knees and calves while walking at a brisk pace may be too much for someone people to accomplish at one time. By combining the two activities, you can decrease the amount of time you participate thus making it easier on those who find it difficult to walk or jog for very long at one time.

Does that mean you can combine jogging with a leisurely walk? That depends on what you are expecting from the jog. A leisurely walk will provide some benefits but not as many as a brisk walk. A leisurely walk is not likely to increase your heart rate and thus will not provide the entire required amount of exercise a person needs on a daily basis. This is especially true for those who are walking or jogging along with a weight loss plan. In order to gain the benefits of aerobic exercises it is important to have a certain momentum along with speed. You might slow down your jog to a brisk walk but you do not want to turn it into a leisurely walk. If you want a leisurely walk, which is very good exercise as well, you want to do that at another time.

Being able to combine brisk walking with jogging with also help prevent some of the problems that are associated with jogging. Not everyone experiences any of those problems but if you already have calf or knee problems, you can minimize any future potential problems if you use the combination of walking and jogging.

Jogging or Running: What Difference Does it Make?

When it comes to exercise, does it really matter if you jog or if you run? Perhaps in theory, it does not make a difference but in reality, you are much better off with jogging. Why is that you may ask? When you run, you tend to begin fast, slow down or stop when you tire, then attempt to pick up speed again. The problem is that you have lost momentum by that time and most likely do not have the ability to regain the power you had in the beginning. You will therefore tire easier and take longer to recover yourstrength and momentum.

Jogging on the other hand allows you to maintain a slow pace from the start therefore, you are less likely to slow down and stop forcing you to lose your momentum. In that respect, you will be in a better position to not only benefit from the jogging itself, but also to be able to use it to boost the metabolic system so it can burn calories. That is not to say that you cannot accomplish it with running but the fact that you tend to slow down and stop more often while you are running makes it less desirable as an activity for burning calories. Running is good for exercising the legs but as a way to boost the metabolism and burn calories the slow but steady pace of jogging is much better.

Of course, some people prefer to engage in a combination of running and jogging and for them the effect is the same. Because you are still jogging you will be able to get the metabolism running while at the same time keeping up your momentum going with jogging. When you combine running and jogging,you have less of a tendency to slow completely down as you do with a steady run. Therefore, you are able to keep the momentum at steadier pace though not as steady as it would be if you were only jogging. You can still gain many benefits from the combination of running and jogging, especially if you allow yourself to maintain timeliness and not just take a few minutes and quit. Build up to an hour a day and you will soon see a big difference in the way you feel in general, look and feel about yourself and your life.

Jogging, Running and Walking, the Aerobic Threesome

When it comes to aerobic exercise, jogging is only one of the three common ones. The combination of jogging, running and walking will go together to form a perfect threesome in the world of aerobic exercise. It is important to understand the importance of aerobic exercise with the most important being its ability to increase the body's metabolism thus making it easier to burn calories. That in itself is a condition for a healthy body since that means either the body will be able to maintain a healthy weight or help a dieter burn fat faster in order to burn more calories than he or she consumes.

Since the fat burners are the aerobic exercises, it makes sense that running, walking and jogging are the perfect combination. Being able to participate in all three throughout the day will make the job easier, especially if one participates in brisk walking as opposed to leisurely walking. Participating in these three aerobic exercises guarantees that you do not become tired or bored with any one activity and are able to continue working on your exercise routine. Of course, you can also add in skiing, bicycling and swimming in order to provide an all around group of fun aerobic exercises.

Choosing from several different exercises in addition to jogging can provide the perfect balance of exercise to boost the metabolism. Whether you are trying to just remain healthy or lose weight you still need to learn how to burn calories or you will gain weight. The body must burn calories that are equal to what you consume in order to maintain your weight or burn more than you consume in order to lose weight. That makes it difficult unless you do exercise that help the body burn those calories. Most people consider jogging to be a fun activity, but you also have to make sure you do it safely with properly fitting shoes and in a safe area.

Combining jogging, running and walking are a good combination for anyone wishing to either maintain or lose weight. You do not have to be on a diet to want to burn fat - you may just need to tone parts ofyour body. Jogging provides that as you swing your arms as you jog along your designated track or trail. The more rhythmic your movements are the more likely you are to burn more calories.

Will Jogging Make Bad Knees Worse?

You hear a great deal of information about jogging causing knee problems. What about those who already have knee problems, will it make them worse? Is there a way to prevent knee problems when you jog? One of the best ways to prevent knee problems when you jog is to make sure you wear the right kind of shoes. You do not want to go to the department store and buy some cheap street sneakers; you want to choose athletic shoes that have specific design for running. Some people prefer cross trainers that are for many different activities but when it comes to jogging, it might be better to choose a running shoe.

If you already have bad knees you may want to consider another activity. Jogging in itself can cause problems with your knees if you are not careful; therefore attempting to jog when you already have badknees may be courting disaster. You want to protect your knees from any further damage by making sure you do not participate in any activity that will cause additional damage. For those with bad knees walking may be better than jogging because of the reduced stress on the knees. It might not be exactly what you want to do, but you have to decide between walking and causing additional damage to your knees. If you make the wrong choice you may end up having knee surgery with no guarantee the problem will correct permanently.

Most joggers who have knee problems developed knee problems after they began jogging. In many cases, it is because of the stress placed on the knees while jogging. In other cases, bad knees result from improper fitting shoes, especially from the era when sneakers were the only form of athletic wear that was available. There were no specially made athletic shoes for running, only for sports like football, basketball, baseball and golf. Running shoes is new on the market when compared to how long jogging and track have been activities. Thus, many of the people who have knee problems related to jogging are older people who began jogging before running shoes were available or at least before people were aware of the importance of wearing running shoes. Today those people are suffering from knee and calf problems, many unable to even walk any more than around their homes and to the store.

Jogging Your Way to a Healthier You

Everyone needs to get into the routine of doing some kind of exercise in order to remain healthy. For some people, that involves developing a jogging routine while others may choose a different kind of exercise. Although jogging is not for everyone, some people are quite content with this activity. Unlike running, when you jog you are at a slower, rhythmic pace which makes it possible to jog for longer than you can run. Though some people are able to run at a slow gait, most people tend to begin running at afast pace and slow down or stop when they get tired then pick up speed again. That type of routine can tire you out quicker and prevent you from accomplishing everything you want to accomplish.

Before you begin jogging you want to decide where you want to jog, keeping in mind that you need to choose a safe and well-lit area that has a level and smooth surface. Once you know where you can jog with confidence, you can begin working on the routine you want to accomplish. Keep in mind you want to start slowly and gradually build up to where you want to be. If you want to jog for an hour a day, do not attempt to begin with that but rather start slowly and build yourself to that level. At the same time, you do not want to push yourself to reach your goal in a week or two - let your body guide you and help you reach your final goal. There is no need to be in a hurry to reach your final goal; you have reached this point in your life without jogging so take it easy.

As you are working toward your final goal be realistic in your expectations. You might want to begin with fifteen minutes and increase it gradually. The idea is to reach your final goal, not to give yourself excruciating pain so that you cannot move. Being in pain from jogging is certainly not the way to begin enjoying this or any other activity. When you begin slowly so that you do not experience substantial pain, you will be more likely to want to continue jogging. Most people will not return to an activity that causes them pain on a regular basis. Gradually increasing the amount of time you spend jogging will help you reduce that possibility.

Let Your Own Body Be Your Guide

One of the most important things to remember about jogging is to let your body tell you when you have had enough. It does not matter if you have only been jogging for fifteen minutes; if your calves and knees are beginning to hurt, you need to stop for the day. You may think you will not experience any lasting effects if you continue but the truth is you can do severe damage to your knees and calves unless you list to your body. Even if you have been jogging for years, you need to stop if you begin to hurt because there may be a reason your body is sending your messages.

One problem that is adamant is that many people still want to live by the adage "no pain no gain,' but time has shown that if you abide by that premise you will do your body more harm than good. People have damaged their legs and knees beyond repair by continuing to exercise when they should have already stopped. You may think you are taking the easy way out, but in reality, you are protecting your body from further damage. Once you damage your muscles or cartilage and continue to exert pressure on that tissue, you run the risk of doing permanent damage.

Allowing your body to be your guide is not something you just do when you begin jogging but something you need to follow anything you participate in that or any other exercise activity. You need to allow yourbody to tell you when it has had enough and when it has to ability to continue. The choices you make will have a long-lasting impact on the activities you will be able to perform during your life and thus the decisions you make regarding your jogging routines should take all of this into consideration. You only get one body and therefore you need to take care not to damage any of its internal components including muscles, bones and cartilage.

Another mistake people make is thinking they need to make up any hours they missed if they were ill or otherwise unable to participate in their regular jogging routine. This will put extra stress on your knees and calves and should be avoid at all costs. This is true not only of jogging but of any aerobic or resistance exercise routine. The worst thing you can do for your body is to attempt to make up for lost exercise time.

Locating the Perfect Place to Jog

It is important to have a good place to jog, somewhere that is safe and has good, solid ground. You donot want to be on hills or rough terrain because that will be detrimental to your legs and will make it more difficult for you to perform as you would like to do. Trying to jog on a hill at the same time will also cause problems with your jogging routine and could also make it difficult for those who have difficulty climbing hills without jogging. It is important to choose an area that makes it easy to jog, is safe and allows you the opportunity to pace your routine so that you do not have to overexert yourself.

Although it may seem that parks offer a good layout for jogging, you have to make sure you are careful in choosing. If the park is in use as a children's playground, it may not be as level as it should be to make a good jogging trail. In addition, you may find playground equipment that is in the way and will not allowyou to jog in a straight line, the preferable means for a good healthy jog. You may also find other rough spots such as rocks and dirt piles that will have a detrimental effect on your routine. In addition, you run the risk of tripping and falling or stumbling while you are jogging. All of these lend way to the possibility of injury.

When looking for the perfect jogging spot you want first to choose an area with a trail that is level and smooth. It will be almost impossible to jog on ground that is rough and uneven. Not only will it make it difficult for you to jog but it may also cause injury to your legs and knees. If possible, choose a soft surface though not one that is so soft that it inhibits your ability to jog. A track that is customarily used for running is the perfect solution, but you also want to make sure of the surface if there has been a great deal of rain or if it is cold outside. Not everyone is close to a school or college where there is a track, and if they are, it may not be available for the public to use, so you want to choose something thatis as close to that environment as possible.

Make Jogging a Group Activity

Quite often, when friends get together they are at a loss for something to do. They have done everything and want something different they have never tried, why not make jogging a group effort? Get some friends together and go for a jog in the neighbourhood, the park or the local track. Not only is it a healthy change from going to the ice cream shop but you will be safer in a larger crowd. Although experts recommend at least two people, the more people who are with you when you jog, the safer youwill be. By making it a group effort you will be both safe and healthy simultaneously.

Whether you arrange jogging as a group with just friends or participate in a sponsored event is of no relevance. The important issue is taking the time to participate in a group jog with friends or with another group of people. Certainly, it is likely to be more exciting if you are with friends but if that is not possible, do not eliminate the possibility of participating in an activity that is already organized. Do not deny yourself the pleasure of joining in a group jog just because you do not know any of the other participants. Events of this type are the easiest way to meet new people and make new friends.

If you cannot find an event that is already sponsored there is no reason y9ou can't get something started yourself. All you need to do is find a group of people interested in joining in a group jogging activity. You can do it like a game or simply provide healthy refreshments at the end of the job. It is not something that needs a great deal of effort or requires a lot of time to organize. You can send flyers around your neighborhood to let everyone know about the event and see how much interest you can generate. The more people that are interested, the more likely it will be of being successful.

You don't have to participate in a group jogging effort of course, but getting together with a group of friends or others who enjoy jogging can make the time go faster, and you will have accomplished your goal before you realize it. When you make it fun the time goes quickly and you can accomplish more, even beyond the original goals you set for yourself.

Protect Your Knees with Proper Shoes

There are special shoes for jogging and other similar exercises. In order to protect your knees you should make certain you wear the proper shoes and that they fit properly. Cross trainers are good for most running and jogging but you may want to ask someone who is experienced in that area if they are right for you. It will depend how much you jog and the kind of ground on which you jog that will make the difference. You do not want to ruin your legs and knees and thus have to give up jogging completely.

Keep in mind that jogging is not good for everyone and for some people simply walking at a brisk pace is the best form of exercise. If you have injured your knees in another activity in the past, you may wish to avoid jogging. The additional pressure to the knees can add additional injury to any you already have. Be safe and be cautious in not only the jogging itself but the shoes you wear when you participate in the activity. Never attempt to jog in regular street shoes or your bare feet. You need the support that is available with sports shoes, preferably one that offers cushioning so you do not come down hard on theballs of your feet and cause damage to your feet.

If you want to continue jogging and even doing other types of exercises that require the use of your feet and knees it's important to make certain you wear proper shoes while you are performing the activity. In addition, if you jog frequently you also want to make sure your shoes fit properly and are in good condition. Most doctors recommend buying new shoes every 8 months - more often if you work on your feet or frequently exercise. No matter how tight your budget may be do not skip on jogging shoes or you run the risk of ruining your feet and your knees. If you have a tight budget look for sales on good shoes rather than skimping and buying jogging shoes that are of a low quality.

For the jogger shoe quality and durability is essential, as is the type of shoe you wear when you are jogging. An ordinary sneaker is not for jogging and will do your feet more harm than good. Consult with a professional in order to choose the shoes that will provide the best protection when you are jogging.

Running or Jogging: the Choice is Yours

Although many people enjoy jogging, others are content with just running or even brisk walking. What is the difference between running and jogging? The major difference is the rhythmic and controlled pace compared to running which tends to have little rhythm to it. While the runner may slow down or even stop every few miles, a jogger tends to go at a steady pace during the entire activity. One of the reasons this may happen is because the jogger maintains a steady slow pace while the runner tends to start out running fast and slows down or stops when he is unable to maintain that pace.

The key is to do what is comfortable for you, but if you want to maintain a regular exercise routine, jogging is better for you than running. That does not mean running is bad but it is more than the short term than the long-term exercise routine. It is more effective to continue at a steady pace instead of changing your pace. This is especially important for those who are unable to run or jog for long periods. Choosing to maintain an even pace throughout your jogging routine will help you keep your heart rate at the same pace and will prevent you from becoming out of breath or overworked. It is much healthier when you can maintain a steady pace instead of trying to make your heart race and maybe faint or develop cramps.

If you enjoy running and jogging, you may wish to alternate your routine in order to incorporate both of the activities. Keep in mind that you are more likely to last longer during your jogging routine, so save your running for those times you may have less time than others are. Running is a good activity to perform in the morning before you go to work though you may choose a leisurely jog as well. The important thing is not whether you run or job but to make sure you protect your feet by wearing properly fitting shoes that have a design for jogging. It also means replacing your athletic shoes on a regular basis and not waiting until they are ready for the trash before you do so. Another mistake many people make is to continue jogging when they are experiencing pain in their knees or legs - stop if you are in pain or you will pain a higher price later.

Safety Tips for Joggers

No matter what time you jog or where you go there are important safety tips you should always follow. Although one usually thinks of these as important for women, men can become victims of crimes just as easily as women can. In most cases one thinks that women are victims of rape while men might be subject to muggings but there is no iron clad rules that will define one gender being more or less vulnerable than the other. Your vulnerability depends upon where you go and how you present yourself.

One of the most important safety tips to follow when jogging is to go with a friend. Even during the daylight, it is a good idea to have someone else with you even if it is only to make sure nothing happens to you or to keep an eye out for someone who looks suspicious. Having someone else with you is usually a deterrent to criminals because they do not want to someone else to see them and be able to report the incident. Certainly, there are exceptions to the rule but in most cases; a criminal will not bother someone who is with another person. They do not want to be identified and though they might attempt to attack and kill someone who could be a potential witness, they realize that person may be able to disappear and notify the police quicker than they can attack.

Avoid using a personal stereo when you are jogging, especially at night. Although you may think it helps you keep your pace better when you have music playing, you are also allowing the music to distract you from things that surround you. You cannot devote your full attention to your surroundings if you have headphones on or ear buds in your ears. Criminals know this and they are always on the lookout for those who do not have their full attention on their surroundings. While you are busy jogging to the music, someone can come out from the bushes, grab you and rape and/or attack you.

Always jog in well-lit and populated areas. It is certainly enticing to jog in the park at night where no one can see you in your sweats or shorts and without your hair and makeup on, but that is very dangerous. Never jog anywhere that you cannot see and hear what is going on around you no matter how safe you may feel. Failure to exercise caution can make you a target for a criminal who may be hiding in the bushes or a dark alley.

Should You Jog when You're Pregnant?

The doctor will tell any pregnant patient to make sure to exercise. However, is jogging an option. The key is whether you were jogging before you got pregnant. Except in rare cases, the doctor will tell a pregnant patient to perform any exercises she performed before she got pregnant but not to start anything new. Of course, that also depends on the weight, age, and health of the mother-to-be, and is something to decide between patient and doctor. There may be any number of reasons a doctor may wish a patient to avoid jogging, so do not assume you can continue to do so without consulting with your doctor first.

Jogging is a very slow rhythmic gait, so in most cases pregnant women can participate as long as their doctor agrees. The farther along you get the more difficult it will become, possibly causing bouncing around of the tummy and thus the baby. Be cautious and sensible when you choose exercise to perform while you are pregnant. Certainly walking is always acceptable, so if you are unable to jog or your doctor does not allow you to do so you can certainly walk. As healthy as jogging is, you do not want to override your doctor and jog if he or she feels you should not do so. No one knows your pregnancy better than your doctor does, so you need to put your faith in those decisions and not assume to know more than the doctor. Remember, it is only for a few months and then you can return to your jogging routine.

Most likely, in the very early stages of pregnancy there is no reason not to participate in jogging. However, as your stomach swells it is less likely you will even feel comfortable attempting to jog. You will have too much of a bulge for it to feel comfortable and will more than likely feel uncomfortable walking let alone jogging. Exercise during pregnancy provides a smoother and easier labor so do not allow being unable to job to deter you from walking. You need to move around and keep limber in order to ascertain you will have an easier delivery. At the same time, you want to choose something that is not going to cause any problems with the baby or your pregnancy thus following your doctor's advice should always be on your agenda for the day.

The Health Benefits of Jogging

Everyone needs to exercise in order to maintain good health. That does not mean you need to spend hours in a gym every week by any means. Some people are not into the gym and for them jogging on a daily basis is the perfect exercise routine. It accomplishes what the exercise intended to accomplish, increase the heart rate and metabolism. Even if your weight is within the normal range, you want to make sure your exercise routine increases the speed of your metabolism so that your weight will remain within the normal range. Of course for those who wish to lose weight there is a need to burn more calories than you consume.

Though it may seem minor to those without a weight problem, exercise is very important. In order to remain healthy you need to exercise enough to increase the heart rate and increase the rate at which your body burns calories. Even without increasing your food intake if you fail to burn off the calories you consume you will begin to gain weight. This is one of the reasons people question why they are not eating any more yet they are gaining weight - a sedentary lifestyle does not leave room for calorie burning.

An added benefit that may not occur to everyone is when you are participating regular in an exercise routine such as jogging you tend to be more conscious of the food you eat. Instead of lying around and munching on chips and other unhealthy foods, you have a greater tendency to choose foods that are good for you. It may be something within the subconscious that makes us do it, but exercise just seems to make us more aware of what we put into our bodies. That is certainly not true of everyone but many people do subconsciously eat better when they take the time to exercise regularly.

How often should you jog? It is a personal decision but if possible, you should jog for at least a half to forty-five minutes every day. If you do not have that much time at once, you can break it into fifteen to twenty minute intervals. Some people use their lunch break to exercise but you have to keep in mind even for short jogs you still need to make certain to wear properly fitting and appropriate shoes in order to avoid damaging your feet, legs and knees.

Using a Track or Jogging Trail

If you are trying to make a decision about whether to jog on an ordinary jogging trail or on a track thereare some things to take into consideration. A jogging trail can consist of anything from a park to the sidewalk in your neighbourhood. When you look at the difference, it is easy to see which one is preferable. It may also consist of broken sidewalk, hard surface and even hills. All of these will make it very difficult and maybe even create hazards that you do not see before an injury occurs.

A track on the other hand consists or dirt or other soft surface and is within a definite area. You know where to go and the length of the track. You do not have to worry about being lost or out after dark in a remote area on which you have no knowledge. The problem is that many people do not have the convenience of being close to a track or are not able to use the track available. Tracks are most often located on the athletic fields of schools or colleges but they do not always allow the public to use them even for jogging.

Before you begin, a regiment of jogging you may want to decide whether you want to use a track or jogging trail and proceed from there to find a place where you can jog. By choosing your spot before you begin jogging you will have time to locate the right spot for you to perform your activity without having to waste time looking when you get ready to do it. If you anticipate needing more than one location, you want to include that as part of your research as well. Before you begin jogging, you should have several places lined up for your activity.

If you are unsure if you want to use a track or trail, take some time and try both - see which one provides the most comfort. It is always good to take the time to do a "trial run" before you are ready to develop your routine. You want to allow yourself enough time to gather the information you need and discover which options will work better for you. Some people like the softer track while others prefer the firmer trail when they are ready to perform their jogging routine.

Lightning Source UK Ltd.
Milton Keynes UK
UKHW020633281222
414497UK00025B/385